FRENCH PAINTINGS
OF THE SEVENTEENTH AND EIGHTEENTH CENTURIES

MUSEUM OF FINE ARTS, BUDAPEST

FRENCH PAINTINGS OF THE SEVENTEENTH AND EIGHTEENTH CENTURIES

by Ágnes Szigethi

CORVINA PRESS

Original title:
FRANCIA FESTMÉNYEK A XVII. és XVIII. SZÁZADBÓL
Corvina, Budapest, 1975

Translated by
ELISABETH HOCH
Translation revised by
BERTHA GASTER
Jacket, cover and typography by
LAJOS LENGYEL
Colour plates from the archives of Corvina Press, Budapest
Photographs by
ALFRÉD SCHILLER

ISBN 963 13 4040 6
Printed in Hungary, 1975
Kossuth Printing House, Budapest

French painting before the nineteenth century still fails to share the popularity enjoyed by the Italian and Spanish schools. Today it is primarily associated with the brilliant painting that headed the evolution of European painting in the nineteenth and twentieth centuries, and which, to a certain extent, has outshone the earlier periods. Yet the way to French hegemony in the nineteenth century had been paved by the course of development of earlier centuries. The continuity of this development marked by a series of real masterpieces, is rightly emphasized by the modern art historians of France. True, not every phase of it is sufficiently well-known; in fact, as we go back in time, each phase becomes increasingly obscure. The inequitable treatment received by these works from posterity is evidenced by the fact that no other field of European painting has called for a similar degree of re-evaluation.

The seventeenth and eighteenth centuries play an exceptionally significant role in this development, a role extending beyond the limits of French art and French culture as such. This period of French history saw years of struggle for the stabilization of the royal power, undermined by half a century of religious strife. They cover the reign of Louis XIII, the regency of Anne of Austria, and the dominance of Richelieu and Mazarin, in the second half of the century, Louis XIV and the establishment of his long reign as an absolute monarch, during which the kingdom of France achieved a leading position among the European states; and finally, in the eighteenth century, the fall of the monarchy and the Revolution. These two great and fertile centuries of French art and culture represent a glorious period of development in painting, stretching from Poussin to David, a period in which the variety of styles is much greater than is suggested by the work of these two men of genius, nearly two centuries apart in time, yet possessing kindred characteristics. The century of Poussin is also that of Valentin, Georges de La Tour, the Le Nain Brothers and Charles Le Brun. It is followed by the new style of painting in an age which was radically different, the age of Watteau, Boucher, Chardin and Fragonard. The painting of the seventeenth century, deservedly called "the Great Century", was more austere, serious and reflective than the eighteenth century, which radiated a sense of serenity, a carefree zest and feeling for the sensuous aspects of existence. It is frequently compared to our own age in terms of human thinking. The man of the Enlightenment, with his ideal of "the honest man" inspired by Cartesian thinking and the morality of Pascal, became increasingly aware of a sense of responsibility as he turned to analyse questions of social justice and equality. The achievements in art which, in addition to setting the fashion for things French in the royal and princely courts of Europe in the eighteenth century, laid the foundations of the supremacy of nineteenth-century French painting, were due to the "Great Generation" of painters who flourished around 1620 and later.

"This was the moment the School as such became self-aware", writes Charles Sterling at the beginning of the century. "It is perhaps the most important period, in which French painting developed into a proper school, a homogeneous, organic whole", says Bernard Dorival in defining the role of the century. And indeed, the significance of the seventeenth century in the history of French art cannot be over-emphasized. The characteristics which French and foreign critics regard as proper to, and determining the nature of French art clarity and simplicity, a feeling for intimacy and an inclination towards intellectual concentration, a moral outlook arising from the prevailing moral code, Rodin's "humility and moderation", have perhaps never been more positively embodied in French art than in this century of European Baroque. Though its formal elements, the turbulence and passion of the Baroque style derives from, and radiates Italian painting, asserted themselves in the art of French contemporaries, Claude Vignon, Simon Vouet, Jacques Blanchard and Valentin, and even in the early style of Nicolas Poussin, it unquestionably evolved in a more balanced, moderate and reserved style than Italian, Flemish or Spanish Baroque. These French painters were contemporaries of Descartes, whose rational outlook and search after truth pervaded the whole intellectual life of the age, and it equally found expression, if at different individual levels and in varying measure, in the art of painting. It was the noble and lofty intellectual aspirations of the first half of the century which inspired the French painters who—like Corneille and Racine in literature—gave a clear shape

6

to the passionately sought balance between moderation and harmony, thought and feeling, within the framework of a wide range of styles expressing what is usually called the classical ideal of the age. "Classical" here means more than a style; Georges de La Tour, Louis Le Nain, Philippe de Champaigne were as much representatives of Classicism, as Nicolas Poussin or Claude Lorrain. The generation that followed in the second half of the seventeenth century, basing itself on the work of this "Great Generation", independent, observing only its own laws, codified, as it were, their doctrine which after Charles Le Brun's austere and lofty interpretation of it gave way to a new approach expressing a desire for relaxation, serenity and gaiety; the mark of the Baroque became more pronounced in French painting at the same time paving the way for the advent of the Rococo period.

All this was of course more complicated than it sounds. Contrary trends continued to exist at the same time, and the transformation of styles was a process that took considerable time. This is not the place to survey the whole complex development of seventeenth and eighteenth-century French painting. In this brief account of its main phases and characteristics we have tried to help the reader to an understanding of the historical position of the old French paintings preserved in our collection as a part of the French painting of these two centuries as a whole.

A discussion of almost any seventeenth-century master could begin with the words "after his death his name and art sank into oblivion, only brought to light again by twentieth-century research". Georges de La Tour, Trophime Bigot, Claude Mellan, Charles Mellin are extreme examples. Thorough investigations into the art of painting in that period have been going on now for almost half a century, and have gradually opened the way to a better knowledge of seventeenth-century French painting and greatly altered our earlier ideas on the subject. The view adopted earlier that nothing important had happened before the "Great Generation" appeared between 1620 and 1630 "from the void" is now outdated. It is evident today that in the simpler and clearer designs produced by Dubreuil,

Fréminet, the members of the second School of Fontainebleau, and by Quentin Varin, the first painter to encourage Poussin, the classical proclivities of the following generations were already taking shape. The artistic development of Frans II Pourbus, who came from Mantua, and whose strictly composed *Last Supper* made a deep impression on the young Poussin, also points in the same direction. The young painters grew up in the tradition of the School of Fontainebleau whose style— "imported" by the Italian Rosso and Primaticcio, but transformed under the influence of French taste—pervaded the art of the whole century. This connection safeguarded a unity and continuity in the development of French painting from the Middle Ages to the seventeenth century or—since the continuity has not yet been broken—to our own days.

Geographically France is situated between the Netherlands on the north and Italy and Spain on the south, with the north-south traffic routes between them traversing her territory. Italian and Netherlandish influence can be continuously felt in her painting, if in varying degrees. In the first quarter of the eighteenth century a number of Italian and Netherlandish painters came to Paris, among them such outstanding masters as Orazio Gentileschi and Rubens, the latter to paint the famous series of the life of Marie de' Médici for the Luxembourg Palace. The invitation to carry out this large-scale work is usually produced as evidence that there was no suitably talented artist among the French painters of that time, and this was indeed so; the young were in Rome, where Simon Vouet's great canvas, *The Birth of the Virgin* for the church of San Francesco a Ripa was already completed, and it was only a few years later that Poussin and Valentin were to paint the large altarpiece for Saint Peter's. The brilliance of Rubens's freely flowing style and his virtuosity were foreign to his French contemporaries; his influence was only to gain ground towards the end of the seventeenth and in the course of the eighteenth century. The young French painters were in quest of something else, and they were not satisfied either by the light, bright, linear style Gentileschi could offer them; they were all anxious to get to Italy, where a world of antique and Renaissance art was lying open to those thirsting for new ideals and new experiences. At the beginning of the seventeenth century artists thronged to Italy, especially to the Eternal City, in unprecedented numbers. The artistic life of Rome, vigorous and lively, the large-scale building activities of the Church, started during the Counter-Reformation (no other period has ever left the mark of its style on the development of the city as incisively as the Baroque), offered great opportunities to painters as well as to architects. The largest group of foreigners assembled here was that made up of the French and Netherlandish artists. The increasing demands for medium-size pictures and the growing number of clients commissioning and collecting this form of art and expanding the market for pictures designed for private use, proved most advantageous to these foreign artists. It allowed them to create an independent position in society for themselves, in many respects very like that held by them at present. Some of the French painters turned their expert knowledge to commercial profit: Claude Vignon, for example, was a recognized expert on paintings and maintained extensive relations with the artists of his age. Nicolas Régnier traded in pictures and assembled in Venice a large and important collection which included pictures by Dürer and his contemporaries, besides works by Titian, Tintoretto, Giorgione and other Venetian masters. (It is interesting to note that the portrait of a woman of the Farnese family, now in the Budapest Museum and earlier attributed to Titian, is in all probability the "Tiziano" once in Régnier's collection, described in his inventory as the portrait of the widow Clelia Farnese.)

In addition to Valentin, Poussin and Claude Lorrain, who made their home in Rome, Tournier and Vouet, together with a host of other artists, some of whom have only been retrieved from undeserved oblivion by recent research, also spent several years in Rome. Many others may have been lost for ever, as a result of the absence of any interest shown in the two centuries that followed. French painters in Italy were not exclusively drawn to Rome: Jacques Blanchard was attracted above all by the colourism of Venice, while Jacques Callot and Jacques Stella worked for many years at the Grand-ducal Court in Florence. The first half of the century, indeed saw what was almost an exodus of French painters. No doubt there were many visiting Italy whose journeys went unrecorded. An eighteenth-century source mentions Georges de La Tour as a pupil of Guido Reni's; an eighteenth-

9

century record distinguishes Louis Le Nain from his two brothers by adding the adjective "Le Romain".

The fresh and original aspects of Italian painting—the qualities so keenly sought by the European painters of the age—exercised a varying influence on French artists. With some of the painters Vouet for example—, the many different influences that inspired them are clearly recognizable; with others, like Le Nain or La Tour, the painter's very individual style completely conceals them. These artists—members of one of the most versatile generations of French painters—were consistent in developing their own distinct and individual style, despite their eager responsiveness to foreign influences.

During the reign of Louis XIII, and especially under the leadership of Richelieu, the domestic stability of France was such that the arts could again flourish and develop. Paris regained its role as the centre of the state administration (during the sixteenth century the French kings had lived mainly at Fontainebleau), and accordingly again became the French centre of art. Richelieu's ambition to make France the leading state in Europe included the world of art, and was accompanied by the extensive patronage of artists. From 1620 to 1630, in quick succession, French painters began to return from their Italian pilgrimage. Blanchard and Vignon were among the firsts in 1623 and 1624. Vouet returned at the king's command in 1627 bringing with him a "train" that included a large number of painters. In the earlier histories of French painting this date is regarded as a milestone, the beginning of an era. And indeed, Vouet's return gave Paris a great personality and a born leader, the bearer of a new spirit. During the twenty years that followed his studio enjoyed great popularity. He was commissioned to paint the most important decorative paintings of the period, but most of this part of his work—various series of paintings embellishing Paris hotels or private houses—has been lost. He also played a major role in the formation of the next generation of painters; practically all the famous members of that generation, from Le Sueur to Le Brun, passed through his studio. His style unites Giovanni Lanfranco's poetic elegance and Guido Reni's steady classicism, with the gay and light colours particular to Venice. His manner of painting won him great popularity, for it radiates a zest for life without vulgarity, it is sweeping, yet well balanced, it is at once easy flowing and arresting. A team of assistants in his studio worked with him on the execution of his numerous orders. Vouet's painting and Vouet's influence are represented in Budapest by one of his later works, *Apollo and the Muses* (Plates 1–3); *The Sleeping Venus* (Plate 4) painted by an artist from his immediate entourage; and *St. Cecilia with the Angel* (Plate 5) by one of his unknown followers.

The soft surface, the misty, vibrant atmosphere and the pearly lustre of the pictures of Vouet's younger contemporary, Jacques Blanchard, show both Venetian and Flemish influences. Blanchard's paintings of rounded, full-bodied women, painted in a sensuous and at the same time melancholy spirit, were popular among French collectors. The painterly qualities of his style were also appreciated by later generations. In the famous "Quarrel of Colour versus Design" of the Academy Blanchard, "the French Titian" was ranked among the predecessors of the "colour party". His *St. Jerome* (Plate 6), in the Budapest Museum of Fine Arts, is one of his rare dated pictures consequently provides an essential foundation for the chronology of his œuvre. The novelty of Blanchard's and Vouet's style and the significance of the Italian impact become even more evident if we compare the works of these artists with that of Augustin Quesnel (Plate 7), a member of an old family of artists, who drew on more limited traditions.

At the beginning of the seventeenth century many of the French artists in Rome were greatly influenced by the traditions of Caravaggio. This trend among the French painters sank into such deep obscurity during later periods that the pictures exhibited in Paris in 1934 produced the effect of fresh discoveries. Around 1610 or so the most important transmitter of the legacy left by the great Italian master in Rome was Bartolommeo Manfredi, a painter of Mantuan origin, who popularized the genre picture so beloved of Caravaggio. The French painters followed his example. In his early years in Rome Vouet developed a monumental style full of dramatic tension through the use of strong contrasts of light and shade; in Valentin's and Régnier's paintings the same style appeared, transposed into a more lyrical tone. For Vouet it was only a temporary experiment; and Régnier as well, after moving to Venice, replaced the somewhat melancholic, deeply reflective style of his Roman period (Plates 8–10) by a softer, lighter and more superficial manner of painting. For Valentin the legacy left by Caravaggio developed into a lasting and final means of expression; Valentin was the greatest and most original of those who amplified and extended its range. In his large genre pictures, full of familiar figures from his own Bohemian world of Rome, he combined a dramatic approach with careful psychological analysis. The noble and spiritual character of the "incurably sad" figures in his companies of merry-makers distinguish this French artist from his contemporaries in the Netherlands, producing also genre pictures, but loud and often vulgar in tone. Valentin's later development shows certain classical traits: graceful contours, calm rhythms, and simple forms of composition prevail, perhaps under Poussin's influence. The humble, quiet art of Nicolas Tournier springs from the same source. After spending a number of years in Rome Tournier worked in Toulouse and in Narbonne in the South of France (Plate 11). Despite its individual character, Valentin's style can be traced back to Caravaggio, but the same cannot be said of Georges de La Tour, in whose paintings it is difficult to discern any foreign influences. Light for him was the means of determining forms of geometric clarity. His severity of form, his austerity, the depths of expression in his work, and above all the continuous effort to achieve a final, perfect solution visible in the recurring figures or his repeated compositions, are all classical virtues. His pictures, whether dealing with secular or religious subjects placed in the familiar surroundings of everyday life and personified by simple people, communicate the depth and security of faith nourished by a sort of timeless wisdom. A late echo of this painter's style may be found in the little known work of Michel Gobin, represented in Budapest by one of his rare figure compositions (Plates 12–13).

Nicolas Tournier, Georges de La Tour, native of Lorraine, and the presumably Provençal Bigot transplanted the Caravaggio style into the art of French provincial towns. This trend had no followers in Paris, but the Le Nain Brothers, who moved from Laon to Paris, came close to the French followers of Caravaggio. Although the rediscovery of the brothers preceded that of Georges de La Tour, their art remains more obstinately enigmatic. Written sources record that the three brothers worked together on the same pictures but signed them only with the name Le Nain, and this fact presents a special problem. The Le Nains are generally known as representatives of the French version of "bambocciata" (an expression derived from the nickname given to the Dutch painter, Pieter van Laer, in Rome), that is, a kind of genre painting, where the scenes are usually placed in a landscape—although in fact religious and mythological subjects as well as portraits also occupy an important place in their œuvre. Their genre pictures show no trace of the grotesque as seen in Netherlandish paintings; their ragged peasant figures always preserve their human dignity. Their works, simply composed, executed mostly in white and pale colours, are monumental in conception and are just as important representatives of French Classicism as Poussin, returning to the antique forms, or Philippe de Champaigne's "classic Jansenism".

Nicolas Poussin gave fullest expression to the highest artistic and moral ideals of his age. A far greater body of his work has come down to us than that of any of his contemporaries, with the exception of Claude Lorrain. His name has been honoured by posterity, his prestige has never been destroyed by changes in taste. The Royal Academy of Painting and Sculpture, founded in Paris in 1648, gave his work the highest rank in the official hierarchy while he was still alive, and honoured him as the greatest living master. It would seem, nevertheless, that his reputation has dimmed, not so much in the literature on the history of art, as in the minds of the public. His art which, according to some art historians, had only won him the recognition of his contemporaries on account of what might be described as a form of intellectual snobbery, no longer produces the same impact today as that of Rembrandt, Velázquez or even Rubens. It is indeed a little fatiguing today to give his intellectual concentration, moral austerity and ideals of perfection the attention they deserve, nor does

13

the intricacy of his brilliant technique make things any easier for the spectator. There has hardly been a painter who has made more use of the traditions of earlier and contemporary painting, or used them with greater freedom, than Poussin. He yearned for Rome, which he reached after several unsuccessful attempts at the age of thirty. Here at last was the "antique", the monuments of the Graeco-Roman age and the Renaissance, known to him until then only from engravings. In his early years in Rome he was greatly influenced by Raphael and Titian (Plates 14–16), not so much in terms of technique as in their attitude towards antiquity. They aroused in him an independent and creative power that went far beyond mere formal repetition. He also devoted great attention to the work of his Roman contemporaries: Domenichino, Guido Reni, Pietro da Cortona and Bernini, who interested him in the question known as "affetti". As interpreted in that period, it meant the expression of states of mind and soul, instead of simply human sentiments. The formal inspiration provided by these artists, however, was only faintly reflected in his work, as for instance Guido Reni's coolly geometric forms of composition echoed in the highly poignant painting of the death struggle in his *Massacre of the Innocents*, now at Chantilly; the mother struggling to defend her child and the soldier poised to kill form a single entity, composed in a single powerful sweep, the faces distorted into masks by the extremes of emotion. He painted no more large-scale pictures after the altarpiece of the *Martyrdom of St. Erasmus*, commissioned for St. Peter's in Rome, but contended himself with the possibilities presented by medium-size canvases. He increased the importance of this form of painting by using such canvases to convey the type of lofty messages, which formerly, generally speaking, had only been attempted in large-scale works of art. Before beginning a picture he made careful and elaborate theoretical and practical preparations. He read all the literature available on the subject chosen, he then made a series of studies with the aid of small wax figures moulded and dressed in draperies with his own hands, and he began to paint only after he had, this way, produced the exact composition he wanted. The work absorbed him completely, both physically and mentally. On one occasion he refused to make a painting of Christ carrying the cross, saying that he could not endure the overwhelming pain the painting of this subject would involve. Such a deep absorption in his work claiming the whole of him required mental calm, and for mental calm he needed isolation and independence. He went to Rome prompted by the desire to study the legacy of the great ages of art, and to appropriate from them what he needed, but in the course of time Rome became his refuge, where he could escape tasks unsuited to his gifts, on the one hand, and the intrigues of jealous fellow-painters that had made his Paris stay (1641–42) a disaster, on the other. Though he had promised the king to return, he left France firmly resolved never to relinquish his independence again. "It is a great happiness," he wrote in 1649 to one of his Paris friends who had commissioned many works from him, "to live in a century so rich in important happenings, if you can hide in a recess and watch the comedy comfortably". How similar to Descartes who wrote in the introduction to his famous *Discourse*, during his stay in Holland, that "I shall always be more grateful to those by whose grace I can use my time freely in tranquillity than to anyone offering me the most important post in the world".

Nor is this Poussin's only point of contact with the thought of his great contemporary. The influence of Descartes's philosophy on Poussin's attitude and methods has been dealt with in a series of thorough and subtle analyses by scholars. The representation of natural forms according to geometrical rules, increasingly dominant in his later work, reveals his acceptance of the theory of Descartes that only regular forms are accessible to the human intellect; irregular forms, that is, natural forms, are not. Poussin's active curiosity, his desire for knowledge is also in keeping with the Cartesian thought, continuing at the same time the tradition set by Dürer and Leonardo. On being asked in his old age how he had risen to such a standard of mastery, Poussin replied: "*Je n'ai rien négligé*" ("I have neglected nothing"). And it was indeed so. According to his German contemporary, Joachim von Sandrart, he used to make excursions to the outskirts of Rome with his fellow-painters in order to make studies after nature. Every piece of work from his brush is the product of long and deep concentration. It cannot be denied that there is a sort of sharp chilling air in his expression of human passions, deriving from the clarity of arrangement which recalls the feeling of order in Racine, and from the perfect equilibrium based on the domination of intellect over feeling. But the chill disappears, and the poetic qualities characteristic of his youth come to life again in his late works much akin to landscape painting. In these paintings he attacks the universal problems and the transient nature of human existence, man's place in nature, the unity of existence and non-existence, joy and grief. By the time he reached this stage he was in a position to consider these questions with the wisdom and stoic calm of one beyond the distinctions of "good and evil".

Withdrawn behind his bastions of solitude, the aged Poussin had only one companion in Rome: Claude Lorrain. Art historians maintain that Claude Lorrain realized the same principles in landscape painting—to which he devoted his life—as Poussin had in his figure compositions. By combining Northern and Italian traditions of painting he created a new type of landscape equal to any form of figural art then in existence. His main problem was to capture the effects of changes in light on the landscape, according to the seasons and the time of day. Claude probably had a stimulating effect on Poussin in the 1640s, when Poussin turned increasingly towards the possibilities presented by landscape painting. In so far as form is concerned the landscapes of the two artists show little relationship: Poussin was concerned to express his philosophic ideas, even in his landscapes, while Claude was concerned with a world of bucolic poetry; against Poussin's generally closed and circumscribed compositions, constructed on strictly geometrical lines, the spatial arrangement in Claude's usually wide-ended landscapes fades into an infinite variety of perspectives dissolving in light and air, which in fact disguise the geometrical skeleton. There is peace and quiet in Claude's landscapes, even when populated with the tragic figures of classical mythology. Nothing overshadows the happiness of the lovers in his *Acis and Galathea*, while in Poussin's *Orpheus* the menacing black cloud in the sky, and the whole atmosphere of the landscape suggest impending tragedy. Claude Lorrain is represented in the Budapest collection by *Villa in the Roman Campagna* (Plates 17–18), a masterpiece bathed in golden light, truly a golden light, and not the nacreous colour produced by yellowing varnish.

The influence of Claude continued to survive in French landscape painting (Plate 19), as late as the eighteenth century. After Poussin and Claude, the third outstanding representative of Roman landscape painting was Gaspard Dughet, although his work is nothing like as well known as that of his two illustrious contemporaries. He was the younger brother of Poussin's wife Maddalena, and it was owing to this relationship that he was permitted to study painting under Poussin's guidance, who otherwise did not accept pupils. He provided landscape painting with new insight. In his pictures the landscape loses its timeless immobility and reveals more personal, turbulent and romantic features. They may even have influenced the style of Dughet's master himself whose landscapes of the 1650s were increasingly finer in quality. Dughet's picture in the Budapest collection shows the neighbourhood of Tivoli (Plate 20), a site he loved to paint.

Thus Rome not only inspired but also provided a scene and background of seventeenth-century French painting. And different as their themes of style might have been, the French in Rome were seeking the same ideal of rational order as the French in Paris. The majority of the French painters visiting Rome returned to their native country after a few years' absence. They were lured back by the increased opportunities opening up to artists, and many indeed were formally recalled by the king. The 1630s also saw the return of Sébastien Bourdon and Jacques Stella. Apart from Vouet, who was by then the master of a large and flourishing studio in Paris, the most prominent of the Paris painters were Claude Vignon, the Le Nain Brothers, and Philippe de Champaigne, and a good many young artists of talent, among them Laurent de La Hyre, Eustache Le Sueur and Charles Le Brun, were growing up beside them.

Philippe de Champaigne never reached Rome. He set out from his native town, Brussels, at the age of nineteen with avowed intention of going to Italy, but got no further than Paris, where he made his home. He brought with him from Flanders the realistic, lively interpretation of the world that characterized Flemish painting, but applied it to the outlook and moral standards he learned to know and accept in Paris. The restrained austerity and concentration on essentials, more particularly on the inner essentials of the spirit of his pictures makes them a superb and characteristic expression of seventeenth-century French art. Like most of his contemporaries, he, too, practised various forms of art, but his best was in the field of portrait painting. He was closely associated with Jansenism, the Catholic movement which exercised such great influence on French intellectual life. It accorded perfectly with Champaigne's personality and found an echo in his purity of style and emotional depth of expression. Budapest possesses his *Portrait of Henry Groulart* (Plate 21), and a fine copy of his portrait of the *Abbé de Saint-Cyran*, the great theologian of the age and friend of Jansenius. A sense of human virtues, profound firmness of character and purity of conscience imbue his art with a serene radiance.

Sébastien Bourdon—who later in life worked for many years at the court of Queen Christina of Sweden—brought back with him from Italy a mellow, poetic style expressing a contemplative melancholy. His delicate art, subdued in tone, is well represented by his painting of a populous mythological scene (Plate 22) in the Budapest museum.

Bourdon's light, transparent patches of colour, and the faint outlines that undulate softly in a hazy atmosphere, are in vivid contrast to the clear and firm lines and porcelain-smooth surfaces that intensify the plasticity of the composition in Jacques Stella's work. Of his eight years in Italy six were spent in Florence, in the course of which the accurate drawing and smooth painting of the Florentine Mannerists became an ineradicable part of his own style (Plate 23).

The efforts made to produce crystal-clear forms and a graceful interpretation between 1640 and 1660 —that is, during the minority of Louis XIV, and the ministry of Mazarin—marked the development of a new ideal in French painting, which French art historians have described as "Attic". The name implies that the painters of the period had reached the heights of the most refined art of antiquity, without a direct knowledge of antique forms. One of the representatives of this trend is Laurent de La Hyre, whose work shows definite signs of Stella's influence. La Hyre's early style, full of youthful vigour, still retained certain elements of Mannerism; in his later works accuracy of form, often combined with fidelity to archaeological detail, went hand in hand with a certain emotional reticence. French art historians regard La Hyre's style as the pictorial equivalent of Corneille's in poetry, in which intellect invariably predominates over emotion and sentiment. His early and his mature period are represented in the Budapest collection by two splendid pictures.

While the moderation and clarity of La Hyre produce on occasion a cool, dry effect, the same characteristics in Le Sueur appear in an extremely subtle, ethereal form. Le Sueur was a pupil of Simon Vouet's, and he only discarded the marks of his master's style in the 1640s, under the influence of Raphael's engravings. His mythological pictures are full of a gentle, naive charm, his religious paintings express his deep and sincere religious feelings. Like La Hyre, Le Sueur had never been to Italy, although he had a consuming desire to see Raphael's paintings at first hand. It is evident, however, that French painters no longer needed the direct inspiration of Italian art, for the works of the "Great Generation" were already providing the background and professional knowledge needed by the artist and a foundation on which the next, and even later generations, cherishing the new ideas of purity, clarity and grace, could develop their individual styles with confidence.

Philippe de Champaigne, Jacques Stella, Sébastien Bourdon, La Hyre, Le Sueur and Charles Le Brun made up the "Ancients" who founded the Academy in 1648. The Academy was originally a union designed to safeguard artists' interests by breaking and by passing the guild system, which acted as a brake on new developments and was detrimental to the interests of the younger generation. Later, due to the statutes imposed by Colbert, it became a means of centralization and, like all French academies of the time, provided an official, perfectly centralized form of organization in intellectual life, under one head, and with direct dependence on the king. By setting up a scale of artistic values it determined its own future activity and the further course of development in painting. Its role

19

was extremely important for not only did it take on the responsibility of training the young generation, but it considered this task one of its major aims. The basic concept was that painting should appeal primarily to the intellect and only in the second place to the emotions. A hierarchy of great masters and of the means of artistic expression was also established: the antique masters, Raphael among the dead, Poussin among the living were ranked the highest; and in fact it was Poussin who inspired its fundamental principles. In terms of technique and types, drawing was given precedence over colour, since the former appealed to the mind, and the latter to the feelings. As regards subject-matter, the "historical" subject (which included religious and mythological as well as strictly historical pictures) ranked highest, taking precedence of the still-life, landscape and genre painting which were regarded as inferior. The aim of art was to imitate nature, but it was to be done according to intellectual rules, that is, with due regard to perspective, proportion and composition. The representation of human passions constituted a central question, and an elaborate system was worked out to provide the right solution. The system of training young artists developed at the time is the one still followed by academic art schools to this day. It is designed to give the student an assured knowledge of the elements of his profession; the task of copying the antique is followed by copying modern masters and it is only after this stage is completed that studies after nature and with the live model begin. This system was improved and extended by the French Academy in Rome, founded in 1666, which made the continuous study of Italian art possible for young French artists, guaranteed a continuation of the inspiration given by Italian art, and consequently prevented a hardening of tradition as late as the eighteenth and nineteenth centuries.

From the beginning the direction of the Academy was in the hands of Charles Le Brun who, apart from his talent as an artist, had a gift for organization. From this post he directed and set the course of French painting in the third quarter of the century, the period which coincided with Colbert's term of office under Louis XIV. It was under his direction that art became a splendid political instrument expressing the grandeur of the *Roi Soleil*. The role of the creative artist took on a political flavour: they were to create a brilliant environment and *décor* for the King of France, the most powerful monarch in Europe, which would proclaim his greatness to both his contemporaries and to posterity. Le Brun's greatest achievement was the decoration of Versailles. Sparing no effort and organizing on an immense scale, he orchestrated the great variety of arts needed into a whole, giving his personal attention to even the smallest details of the work. He also developed the allegorical language used in painting to glorify the monarch, claiming for Louis XIV not only a position among the greatest figures of history, but among the gods of Olympus as well. The sense of energy and power suggested in Le Brun's paintings and the loftiness of his style gave perfect pictorial expression to the age of Louis XIV. In his historical pictures, populated by immense crowds, his aim was to catch the passion and sentiment of each individual figure while preserving the unity of the scene. His ambitions as a painter were noble: he was prepared to compete with the most famous masters of the great periods of art. Yet today we find those works most convincing in which he made no pretensions to the spectacular, his magnificently simple portrait of *Séguier* for example, or his late *Adoration of the Shepherds*. The Budapest Museum of Fine Arts possesses one of his allegorical pictures (Plate 27) painted to glorify Louis XIV. It is touched in as swiftly and lightly as a sketch, in a restrained colour-scheme bordering on monochrome, an embodiment of the academic doctrine that colour is only of secondary importance.

Until quite recently the role of Le Brun over the painting of his time has been regarded as that of a despot; today, however, his incontestable merits as a man and an artist are again recognized. As first painter to the king and director of the Academy he enjoyed complete authority, of which he was later deprived by the intrigues of his rival, Mignard, after the death of Colbert. He has been accused of suppressing individuality in contemporary painters. It is, however, beyond dispute that there were few talented artists among his contemporaries. The body of "academician" painters is represented in the Budapest collection by Nicolas Loir, painter of historical subjects (Plate 30), Francisque Millet, who painted landscapes, and Le Brun's confirmed rival, Pierre Mignard (Plate 29).

Even if they fail to give a full panorama of the painting of the age, they are characteristic of its general level. The pictures by Nicolas Colombel and Fouché (Plates 33–34) even suggest that a new movement in art was beginning to appear challenging the strict rules laid down by Le Brun and the insistence on the heroic. Resistance to his doctrine gradually increased until it finally came into the light in the famous academic "Quarrel of Colour versus Drawing" of 1671.

Colour—the question whether colour is really inferior to drawing—was only the subject, not the essence of the debate. The battle of words fought in favour of colour expressed the changed outlook of society, the appearance of new attitudes to art, the fact that the man of the age was weary of heroic glories. What he wanted from art was gaiety and relaxation; he wanted it to appeal to his senses as well as intellect. (Some witty arguments in fact, were adduced in the course of the debate, as for instance, that colour was superior to drawing because drawing appealed only to the expert, while colour appealed to everyone.) All this affected the earlier scale of values: the "colourists", among the old masters, the Venetians, Correggio and in particular Rubens, whose influence now began to bear fruit, returned to favour.

At the same time the style of painting changed; a softer manner of expression, based on Flemish models, more immediately pleasing to the eye, gained ground. The Flemish influence first appeared in portrait painting, regarded at the time as one of the inferior subjects of academic art. The Flemish touch was introduced by Largillière and Hyacinthe Rigaud, who returned to France from the London studio of Sir Peter Lely. Largillière began by following Van Dyck in elegant and accomplished portrait painting, but he replaced the Flemish painter's taste for aristocratic portraits by a feeling for the exuberant joy of life. He loved attractive light and bright colour schemes, and flowing and fluttering draperies; the excessive movement and agitation in his pictures was meant to enhance the decorative effect of his elegant style. Rigaud adopted a similar style of painting, but with greater sobriety and dignity (Plate 35); he refused to flatter or embellish, so it is no mere chance that he had few women sitters. Louis XIV, however, still lives in the mind of posterity as Rigaud painted him

22

in 1701 in his heavy, full-length portrait, in sombre splendour. Eventually his work was in such demand that he organized a studio, staffed with numerous assistants.

The most spectacular change in style took place in the field of decorative painting; in Budapest this development is represented by a painting of Jean-Baptiste van Loo's (Plate 36), one of a large and popular family of artists. Mythology no longer presented the painter with a collection of heroic prototypes, but became a source of themes about love. Antoine Coypel—a sketch of whose masterpiece, the decoration of the ceiling in the Palais Royal, is preserved in Budapest—defined *le grand goût* as a style in which nobility and dignity are guaranteed by both the choice of, and the approach to the subject. Thus far his definition agreed with the principles in acceptance in the preceding century; in so far as form was concerned, however, he declared that dry and harsh effects should be avoided, and the way to do it was to follow Correggio's example and use billowing forms undulating like flames. The demand for pictures with an air of carefree optimism that delighted the eye was gaining ground. To satisfy it French painters sought inspiration from predecessors formerly neglected, such as the painters of northern Italy, Parma and Venice, but also from Flemish artists.

Exhibitions became established events; they helped to develop new forms of relationship between art and the public. Annual exhibitions by the Academy had already been envisaged by Colbert, but only a few took place. In the seventeenth century the public knew what was going on in painting, but in general only from religious works. In addition to the paintings which habitually adorned churches and which were of course accessible to all and sundry, there was the famous annual "May" events when the picture donated each year by the Goldsmiths' Guild to the Cathedral of Notre-Dame was exhibited. From 1630 onward practically every important artist was commissioned to paint one of these pictures. There was no occasion, however, to exhibit paintings of secular subjects, although they were becoming increasingly popular. It was to compensate for this lack of publicity that the "exhibition of young artists" was organized, taking place in the long intervals between academic exhibitions; they were held at the Place Dauphine on Corpus Christi Day, at the time of the religious procession. For lack of other opportunities the Academicians also showed painting at them. Although they were open for no more than a few hours a year, these exhibitions were of considerable importance, since they offered the young a chance to attract attention to their work and distinguish themselves, as in the case of Chardin.

The success of the exhibitions at the Place Dauphine contributed to the revival of the academic "Salon", so called after the Salon Carré in the Louvre where the pictures were generally shown.

The nineteenth-century description of the Academy as a generally reactionary institution will not hold water, for the Academy both recognized and supported the greatest young talents of the period—Watteau, Chardin and Fragonard. Its attitude towards these most outstanding masters of the eighteenth century must indeed be termed loyal since both the choice of their subject matter and the treatment of their material, their approach was far removed from the official trend represented by the academic authorities.

Within the walls of the Academy fierce battles were fought between the partisans of tradition and the supporters of new principles of painting, such as the "Quarrel of Colour versus Drawing" and the "Quarrel of the Ancients and the Moderns" at the end of the century. Both these disputes ended with the victory of the moderns. The second of the two centred on the question as to whether contemporary art should be rated less valuable than the older trends. All these arguments expressed the increased self-assurance of the French painters of the age. The time was not far when they would practically take possession of all the great cities of Europe; French taste became dominant and remained so throughout the eighteenth century.

The demands of the new generation at Court and the upper middle class and noble patrons of art generally underwent considerable changes from the seventies on, shifting from the grand and impressive towards the familiar and intimate, from the strict and heroic towards the sensuous and gay, in fact, towards Rococo. The most poetic interpreter of this transformation was Watteau. Born in the seventeenth century, he was the first great genius of the eighteenth century. Yet his painting expresses a nostalgic farewell to an irrecoverable age in which existence possessed a magical and poetic beauty. He was himself endowed with strongly poetic feelings, and his work shows no respect for academic rules, neither in form, nor in subject. In place of the seventeenth century quest for what was permanent and enduring, he tried to catch the evanescent, the fleeting moment. Though numerous painters before him had taken the world of the theatre as subject matter, their works had all been mediocre. Watteau's personal sense of poetry gave the subject such eloquence that we sometimes have the feeling that the property room of the stage formed his favourite subject, because, modest as he was, under the pretext of "play-acting", he could give to his inner world franker and more undisguised expression. In his ideal of beauty we note a distant reflection of the high-keyed, elegant figures in Bellange's Mannerist paintings, while the far perspective of his vaporous landscapes suggest Claude Lorrain. Watteau drew greatly on the dazzling art of Rubens, the much admired painter of the Marie de'Médici series in the Palais de Luxembourg, though the exuberance and almost rustic vitality in the works of the Antwerp master are in fact very far removed from the ethereal and delicate charm of Watteau. He knew Giorgione's work, and in several of his paintings he revived the atmosphere of Giorgione's *Concert*, but in comparison with the palpable solidity and reality of Giorgione's figures, Watteau's seem to float to the melody of soft music and dissolve into the velvety atmosphere of the background, which in turn is evocative of Titian. The wistful passengers in the *Debarkation from the Island of Cythera* or the figure of *Gilles* in the costume of a role unsuited to him, all represent Watteau's own personal world. The more personal, because he does not paint it as the real and actual world, but as a dream-world, with the sigh that follows the beauty and purity of dreams, knowing they only exist in our world of fantasy. In Watteau's new style, new and perfectly individual, the ideal of restraint and harmony is the same as that of his seventeenth century predecessors. Compared to the earlier ideal of man—resolute in character, prepared for combat—it took on a new character in Watteau, an attitude of resignation and reconciliation connecting with Poussin's line of thought in his later work.

After Watteau, the attitude in eighteenth-century French art, distinguished by an attraction for the beauty of serenity, a carefree existence and the sensuous pleasures of life, became less poetic in its expression and more obvious, exemplified in the first place by the work of the two outstanding Rococo masters, Boucher and Fragonard. This period produced a wide variety of individual artists in terms of style and expression. The two extremes of this range are represented by two contemporaries, Boucher and Chardin, the former with his uninhibited sensuousness, the latter with his attitude of mental detachment. Both Chardin's and Boucher's art, one should note, can only be truly understood in the light of the important social changes that were taking place, and the very different approaches of the different classes of society, soon to confront one another.

Chardin devoted himself to still-life subjects and bourgeois genre paintings as far removed from the official academic formula as was the poetic world of Watteau, which, however, had been accepted by the Academy: the hitherto unknown form of art of *fête galante* was constituted for him. Chardin's beginnings were modest: he studied under Pierre-Jacques Cazes, a mediocre painter who transmitted the influence of the Netherlands. Chardin later became one of those painters filling in the details of other men's work—a task regarded as inferior. Both these facts carried in themselves, at least in part, the seeds of his later development. Nevertheless, his success was surprising, taken the choice of his subject matter, regarded unpromising by his contemporaries and immediate predecessors, and the novelty and radicality of his approach. The young painter's talent was discovered by Largillière at the Place Dauphine exhibition of 1728. He achieved overwhelming success with the Academy and was unanimously adopted as a fellow-member. The fresh pictorial qualities, the simplicity and homely, human atmosphere of his pictures form a link between Le Nain and Cézanne. As he said himself, he used colours, but painted with emotions. This is clear from the tone of both his genre paintings produced between 1730 and 1740, and his still-lifes. The intensity of expression in his genre works springs from the depth of his psychological insight and from his wonderful gift for capturing the fleeting moment; it is the same qualities that give such meaning to the permeating still-lifes (Plate 38).

Boucher's virtuosity, and the elegant, sensuous world he painted were as remote from the simple human world painted by Chardin as the industrious life of the bourgeoisie, devoted to useful work, was remote from the luxurious, pleasure-wearied life of the aristocracy. His serene and easy-flowing style accords perfectly with the mythological subjects he projects so voluptuously. In spirit, and in the pure harmony of his colours, he recalls Tiepolo. He was a splendid "decorator", and aspired to nothing more. His open sensuousness was sharply criticized by Diderot, though Diderot's arguments occasionally raise a smile. Referring to the putti in Boucher's paintings, he protested that "in this large family of children we cannot find one that would pursue a realistic occupation, study his homework, write a lesson or beat a bit of hemp". Similar reproaches, I suppose, could be addressed to the child figures in the works of Rubens, Titian or Poussin.

Numerous portraits of the nobility that commissioned Boucher's paintings have come down to us, both in the traditional oil technique and in the pastel pictures so popular in the eighteenth century (Plates 39–40). It would, of course be useless to seek in the Rococo portraits of the eighteenth century the strict characterization and profound psychological insight found in the works of the previous century. In their portraits, with their velvety surface, which bore witness to their great technical skill, Maurice Quentin de La Tour and Marc Nattier were as much concerned to flatter the model as to produce an effect of discretion and elegance. All these types of painting, however, were distant from what the Academy recognized as the highest form of art, that is, historical painting. Repeated attempts were made to revive it and to bring back the arts unto the service of morality. Success in this direction was achieved by calling on the tradition of the antique and on Italian Baroque art. The first important representatives of the new trend were Joseph Marie Vien (whose pupils included Peyron [Plate 41] and David), and Gabriel-François Doyen. The last—represented by one of his early masterpieces (Plate 42) in the Budapest collection—combined the dynamic style of Pietro da Cortona

27

and Guido Reni with which he had become acquainted during his stay in Italy, with the vigorous painterly qualities characteristic of Rubens. Diderot gave his enthusiastic approval to his work, though his ideal painter remained Greuze, who fully accepted and reflected in his work, the didactic-moralist principles preached by the men of letters and philosophers of the age.

Greuze's pictures—far from the ideal designed to appeal to the mind—appeal above all to the sentiments of the spectator. He drew up detailed literary programmes for his pictures, and put them in the newspapers. His taste for narrative found expression in his studies and portraits of children and women as well as in his genre pictures. With four paintings Greuze is the best represented eighteenth-century French artist in the Budapest collection (Plates 43–44); only examples of his genre paintings are missing. His portrait of Randon de Boisset displays his art at its most attractive and enduring.

Landscape painting also occupied an important place in eighteenth-century art. The greatest masters of pure landscape painting were Joseph Vernet and Hubert Robert. Vernet (Plate 47) took up the threads of the Claude Lorrain tradition, partly through the intermediary of his teacher, Adrien Manglard, and enriched it with effects taken from Salvator Rosa's lively, bustling landscapes. Robert lived in Italy for fifteen years, several of them spent in travel in the company of Fragonard. It is evident that Fragonard's ease of style and passionate calligraphy influenced Robert's early work *Ruins with Figures* (Plate 48), insubstantial in form and bearing the traces of swift strokes of the brush, the only "Rococo" painting in the Budapest collection, but it also gives some idea of Fragonard's style as well.

Fragonard learned his art from Boucher and Rubens. He worked in the studio of the former and studied Rubens's works in the Palais de Luxembourg. Whatever art form he choose, he expressed the same sense of happiness in the unclouded pleasures of life as the masters he followed. The work he submitted to the Academy held out great promise in the field of historical painting, but, instead of seeking the laurels of the Academy, he sought popularity among the connoisseurs. His unmistakably individual style is coloured by many different influences. His *Bathing Nymphs* is evocative of

28

Rubens, but the swirling patches of colour also recall the restless brush-work of the Genoese painter, Benedetto Castiglione. The bold forms of his studies of heads announce Tiepolo's influence, while at the same time anticipating something of the qualities of Daumier. His allegorical love scenes, literary in inspiration, are the forerunners of Romanticism. In reply to the sighing melancholy of Watteau, his paintings affirmed the beauty and pleasures of life.

The many and different trends of French painting in the eighteenth century were by no means incompatible with one another. In our age we are liable to see a conflict between trends and paintings of different character and to regard their styles as mutually antagonistic. To illustrate how simple and natural it was to respect individuality in painting in the eigtheenth century, it is enough to recall that at the time of the Revolution, David, the strict preacher of Roman morals and master of a crystal-clear style, appointed Fragonard, the embodiment of spontaneous painting, as curator of the Louvre, in recognition of his work. And with the close of the eighteenth century two great centuries of French painting came to an end. This rich age concealed within itself the possibility of the re-emergence of the vigour of the glorious great generation, the seventeenth century, and in an intensified and renewed form.

The present volume contains a selection from the seventeenth and eighteenth-century French paintings in the Old Masters Gallery of the Budapest Museum of Fine Arts. The private collections and provincial museums do not, as in the case of the Italian, German and Netherlandish schools of painting, add much to this modest French collection.

The Budapest Museum possesses no examples of earlier French painting from the Middle Ages, and those dating from the Renaissance are of no great artistic significance. The greatest deficiency in the seventeenth and eighteenth-century collection is the absence of paintings by masters of the Rococo.

The majority of the pictures, among them Jacques Blanchard's dated and signed *St. Jerome*, Philippe de Champaigne's similarly dated and signed *Portrait of Henry Groulart*, Nicolas Régnier's melancholic *Card-Players*, Simon Vouet's *Apollo and the Muses*, Laurent de La Hyre's two historical scenes, Claude Lorrain's poetic *Villa in the Roman Campagna* and Charles Le Brun's powerful *Apotheosis of Louis XIV* found their way to the Museum from the former Esterházy Collection, which was bought by the Hungarian State in 1870. The eighteenth century was represented in the same princely collection by Hyacinthe Rigaud's portraits, landscapes by Adrien Manglard, Joseph Vernet and Hubert Robert, a genre picture by Boilly and Greuze's *Portrait of a Young Girl*. This very incomplete list of names does not of course mean that the Esterházys entertained any prejudice against the French. On the contrary: their palace at Fertőd known as the "Hungarian Versailles" was modelled on the famous French palace, as indeed were almost all the royal and princely residences of Europe of the age; a monumental series of allegories representing the four elements were commissioned from the pupils of the French Academy in Rome by Antal Pál Esterházy when he was Imperial ambassador in Naples. Prince Miklós II Esterházy, who founded the family collection of paintings, also bought a number of works alleged to be by Poussin, Valentin, Claude Lorrain, Le Sueur—more than the Museum possesses today, as modern methods of analysis have proved most of them to be by other artists, or simply copies. Prince Miklós III Esterházy wanted an all-round collection. He was a contemporary of Winckelmann and an enthusiastic admirer of Canova and Anton Raffael Mengs; in his artistic tastes he can only be charged with one prejudice: that of Classicism against the Rococo. As a result Rococo painters were consequently missing from his collection, and the gap they left could not be filled, even by the later purchases of the Museum. Apart from this lacuna, the French masters were represented in reasonable proportion in his collection. But as the Museum of Fine Arts developed, much fewer French than Italian and Netherlandish paintings were acquired, and there was a considerable imbalance between the different national schools. Later acquisitions, however, included important items for the French collection too. Chardin's *Still-life with Turkey*, and Doyen's monumental

Juno and Aeolus have filled important gaps in the group of eighteenth-century pictures. Among the seventeenth-century paintings the *Rest on the Flight to Egypt* is exceptionally significant; although doubts on its authorship have been expressed, its style is definitely closely related to Poussin's. Another valuable acquisition is Michel Gobin's *Boy Smoking a Pipe*, an example of a trend little represented in the Museum before.

While the French collection in the Old Picture Gallery may be modest compared to other schools, it is by no means unimportant. It contains works by many great masters, especially from the seventeenth century, which are of definite or even outstanding quality. In addition to these, the paintings of the lesser masters—some of whose works may be regarded as rarities, for example the works of Gobin, Fouché and Bernard—also deserve interest, as do the pictures of hitherto unknown or only vaguely identified painters as their works constitute a promising reserve, possibly adding further names to the catalogue of the Budapest Museum.

BIBLIOGRAPHY

A complete list of references covering the pictures presented in this book can be found in Andor Pigler's *Catalogue of the Old Picture Gallery*, 1954 and *Katalog der Galerie Alter Meister*, Budapest, 1967. The references listed hereunder comprise the more important general literature on seventeenth and eighteenth-century French painting and some more recent literature not included in Pigler's catalogue.

GENERAL LITERATURE:

1925   L. Dimier: *Histoire de la Peinture française : Des origines au retour de Vouet (1300–1627)*. Paris, 1925.

1926/27 L. Dimier: *Histoire de la Peinture française : Du retour de Vouet à la mort de Le Brun*. Paris, 1926–27.

1928   L. Dimier: *Les Peintres français du XVIIIe siècle* Paris, 1928.

1932   W. Weisbach: *Französische Malerei des 17. Jahrhunderts*. Berlin, 1932.

1942   B. Dorival: *La Peinture française*. Paris, 1942.

1953   A. Blunt: *Art and Architecture in France 1500 to 1700*. London, 1953.

1958/60 R. Huyghe: *L'Art et l'Homme*. Vols. II–III, Paris, 1958–60.

1963   A. Chatelet–J. Thuillier: *La Peinture française de Clouet à Poussin*. Geneva, 1963.

1964   A. Chatelet–J. Thuillier: *La Peinture française de Le Nain à Fragonard*. Geneva, 1964.

1965   G. Janneau: *La Peinture française au XVIIe siècle*. Geneva, 1965.

RECENT LITERATURE NOT INCLUDED IN PIGLER'S CATALOGUE:

1934   A. Rostand: "Adrien Manglard et la peinture de marine." *Gazette des Beaux-Arts* (1934), pp. 263–272.

1956   B. Dorival: "Note sur la famille Quesnel, un peintre mythique: Augustin II. Quesnel." *La Revue des Arts* (1956), pp. 236–238.

1962   Th. Augarde–J. Thuillier: "La Hyre." *L'Oeil*, (1962), No. 88, pp. 16–23 and 74–75.

1966   A. Blunt: *Nicolas Poussin. A Critical Catalogue*. London, 1966.

1967   M. Röthlisberger: *Claude Lorrain. The Drawings*. Berkeley–Los Angeles, 1967.

1968/69 *Angelika Kauffmann und ihre Zeitgenossen*. Bregenz – Wien, 1968/69. Catalogue of the exhibition (Peyron).

1969   M. Chiarini: "Alcuni quadri di paesaggio nel Museo di Belle Arti di Budapest." *Bulletin du Musée des Beaux-Arts—A Szépművészeti Múzeum Közleményei* (1969) No. 33, pp. 123–129 and 207–209. (Dughet).

1970   A. Blunt: "Nicolas Colombel." *Revue des Arts* (1970), No. 9, pp. 26–29.

1970   P. Rosenberg–J. Thuillier: "The Finding of Moses by La Hyre." *Bulletin of the Detroit Institute of Art* (1970), No. 2, pp. 26–28.

1971   B. Dorival: "Essai d'identification d'un portrait d'inconnu par Philippe de Champaigne." *Bulletin du Musée des Beaux-Arts — A Szépművészeti Múzeum Közleményei* (1971), No. 37, pp. 45–54 and 111–114.

1972   *Europäische Landschaftsmalerei 1550–1650*. Dresden, 1972. Exhibition catalogue (Claude Lorrain).

1974   *Valentin et les Caravagesques français*. Paris, 1974. (Régnier).

LIST OF PLATES

1 SIMON VOUET
   APOLLO AND THE MUSES

2 SIMON VOUET
   APOLLO AND THE MUSES (detail)

3 SIMON VOUET
   APOLLO AND THE MUSES (detail)

4 SCHOOL OF SIMON VOUET
   THE SLEEPING VENUS

5 FOLLOWER OF SIMON VOUET
   ST. CECILIA WITH THE ANGEL

6 JACQUES BLANCHARD
   ST. JEROME

7 AUGUSTIN QUESNEL
   THE LUTE PLAYER

8 NICOLAS RÉGNIER
   THE CARD-PLAYERS

9 NICOLAS RÉGNIER
   THE CARD-PLAYERS (detail)

10 NICOLAS RÉGNIER
   THE CARD-PLAYERS (detail)

11 NICOLAS TOURNIER (?)
   A PARTY

12 MICHEL GOBIN
   BOY SMOKING A PIPE

13 MICHEL GOBIN
   BOY SMOKING A PIPE (detail)

14 NICOLAS POUSSIN (?)
   THE REST ON THE FLIGHT INTO EGYPT

15 NICOLAS POUSSIN (?)
   THE REST ON THE FLIGHT INTO EGYPT (detail)

16 NICOLAS POUSSIN (?)
   THE REST ON THE FLIGHT INTO EGYPT (detail)

17 CLAUDE LORRAIN (CLAUDE GELLÉE)
   VILLA IN THE ROMAN CAMPAGNA

18 CLAUDE LORRAIN (CLAUDE GELLÉE)
   VILLA IN THE ROMAN CAMPAGNA (detail)

19 FRANCISQUE MILLET
   PASTORAL LANDSCAPE

20 GASPARD DUGHET
   PASTORAL LANDSCAPE

21 PHILIPPE DE CHAMPAIGNE
   PORTRAIT OF HENRI GROULART

22 SÉBASTIEN BOURDON
   BACCHUS AND CERES WITH NYMPHS AND SATYRS

35

23 JACQUES STELLA
   THE MARRIAGE OF THE VIRGIN

24 LAURENT DE LA HYRE
   THESEUS AND AETHRA

25 LAURENT DE LA HYRE
   THESEUS AND AETHRA (detail)

26 LAURENT DE LA HYRE
   CORNELIA REJECTING THE CROWN OF THE
   PTOLEMIES

27 CHARLES LE BRUN
   THE APOTHEOSIS OF LOUIS XIV

28 FRENCH PAINTER. 17TH CENTURY
   PORTRAIT OF A YOUNG MAN

29 PIERRE MIGNARD
   CLIO

30 NICOLAS LOIR
   CLEOBIS AND BITON

31 FRENCH PAINTER. 17TH CENTURY (after Raymond
   Lafage[?])
   CAIN BUILDING THE CITY OF ENOCH

32 FRENCH PAINTER. 17TH CENTURY (after Raymond
   Lafage[?])
   THE BUILDING OF NOAH'S ARK

33 NICOLAS COLOMBEL
   HAGAR AND THE ANGEL

34 NICOLAS FOUCHÉ
   A LADY AS POMONA

35 HYACINTHE RIGAUD
   CARDINAL FLEURY

36 JEAN-BAPTISTE VAN LOO
   APOLLO AND DAPHNE

37 ROBERT TOURNIÈRES
   PORTRAIT OF COUNT FERDINAND ADOLF VON
   PLETTENBERG AND FAMILY

38 JEAN-BAPTISTE SIMÉON CHARDIN
   STILL-LIFE WITH TURKEY

39 PIERRE BERNARD
   PORTRAIT OF A YOUNG MAN

40 PIERRE BERNARD
   PORTRAIT OF A YOUNG WOMAN

41 JEAN-FRANÇOIS-PIERRE PEYRON
   KING PERSEUS BEFORE AEMILIUS PAULUS

42 GABRIEL-FRANÇOIS DOYEN
   JUNO AND AEOLUS (The Allegory of Air)
   (detail)

43 JEAN-BAPTISTE GREUZE
   RANDON DE BOISSET

44 JEAN-BAPTISTE GREUZE
   PORTRAIT OF A YOUNG GIRL

45 LOUIS-LÉOPOLD BOILLY
   VISITING GRANDFATHER

46 ADRIEN MANGLARD
   ESTUARY WITH HARBOUR

47 JOSEPH VERNET
   VIEW WITH CASTLE RUINS

48 HUBERT ROBERT
   RUINS WITH FIGURES

PLATES

I

SIMON VOUET
1590–1649

APOLLO AND THE MUSES

Painted in the late 1630s
Inv. No. 707
Panel, 80 × 221.5 cm
From the Esterházy Collection, 1870

Simon Vouet painted two other versions of the Parnassus with Apollo and the Muses in addition to this picture in Budapest, one for Wideville Castle, the other for the library of the Hôtel Séguier. (The latter has only survived in engraving.) The formal composition of the picture, dominated by yellows and blues, is naturally different from the ceiling paintings composed according to Baroque illusionist principles. In the carefully balanced composition, somewhat akin to a frieze, the rhythmic grouping, the erratically broken draperies of the female figures, and the boldly curving outlines combine to produce the smooth formal sweep of the design and lofty and harmonious overall effect. The single principle underlying this style is decoration in the noblest sense of the word. Stylization in every detail, a broad air of grandeur, healthy, robust, yet noble types of beauty go to produce the decorative effect. The picture shows a strong affinity of style with Vouet's *Diana* at Hampton Court, dated 1637, which indicates that it is a work of the painter's late period. It is fair to assume that it formed part of a decorative series, to which also belong the *Urania and Calliope* in the Kress Collection, the *Polyhymnia* in the Louvre and the *Euterpe* in the Cailleux Collection in Paris.

2

SIMON VOUET

APOLLO AND THE MUSES (detail)

Apollo, gazing upward with enraptured eyes as he plays the lyre and leads the chorus of the Muses, forms a fine curve between the lightly flowing drapery and the delicate lines of the lyre. This detail provides an excellent stylistic example of the balanced and harmonious outlook and "Apollonian" spirit of French Baroque painting.

SIMON VOUET

Apollo and the Muses (detail)

The Muses are sensuous, richly beautiful feminine figures, yet intellectual in character, owing to their meditative expression. On the left Calliope rests her elbow on her books; beside her is Melpomene; behind them Thalia, and further back Terpsichore embracing Euterpe. In the background can be seen the pale silhouette of Pegasus, the winged horse of poetry melting into the cumulus clouds. As Isaac Habert describes it in his poem on Dorigny's engraving of the ceiling of the library in the Hôtel Séguier, this is the Parnassus, the happy home of the Muses, where they bestow poetic inspiration on those who drink from the inexhaustible spring.

FOLLOWER OF SIMON VOUET

St. Cecilia with the Angel

First half of the 17th century
Inv. No. 67.8
Canvas, 104×98 cm
Purchased from a private collection in 1967

The painter of *St. Cecilia* was greatly influenced by the style Simon Vouet had adopted during his early years in Rome. The characteristic profile—which preserves the features of Virginia da Vezzo, the artist's Italian wife—the childish face of the angel, the dimpled hands with long tapering fingers, are all elements characteristic of Vouet's art. The painter obviously took pleasure in lingering over many of the decorative details, and especially in displaying the varied effects of the drapery. His more detailed presentation, however, fails to equal Vouet's bold simplicity, and his drier and more broken outlines compare unfavourably with the calm flow of the master's painting, nor does the strong alternation of light and shade produce the powerful modelling we are accustomed to see in Vouet's works. But what distinguishes the picture most from Vouet's lofty but natural tone is its theatrical and artificial character, apparent in both the facial expressions and the gestures. This is particularly evident in comparing the picture with Vouet's painting on the same subject in Amiens.

6

JACQUES BLANCHARD
1600–1638

St. Jerome

Painted in 1632
Inv. No. 681
Canvas, 145.5 × 116 cm
Signed on the open page of the book: Jac. Blanchard F 1632
From the Esterházy Collection, 1870, purchased from Artaria art dealers in Mannheim, 1808

This picture of *St. Jerome* represents the highest level of Jacques Blanchard's art. The simply constructed, monumental figure recalls the type of half-length saints painted by the Bolognese Guido Reni, without, however, his ascetic rigour, while the vibrant surface, the lively brushwork and the colours are Venetian in inspiration. Due to his use of impasto in painting, Blanchard was called "the French Titian", and this epithet is misleading only in so far as his paintings were inspired by contemporary rather than Renaissance Venetian art. At the beginning of the seventeenth century Venetian colourism was enriched by the cruder palette of the Northern painters through Domenico Fetti and Johann Lys. The latter was still alive when Blanchard went to Venice in 1626. The most meticulously detailed part of the picture is the silvery head, painted in almost nervous calligraphic strokes, more specially the hair and beard, without breaking the magnificent unity of the overall effect. The face of the meditating saint is calm, even serene; the French painter, well-balanced in his outlook, gave way to none of the exaggerated mysticism commonly found in the religious art of the age. The effect is rich and calm in both expression and colour, yet free from crudity of tone.

8

NICOLAS RÉGNIER
About 1590–1667

THE CARD-PLAYERS

Painted before 1626
Inv. No. 610
Canvas, 174×228 cm
From the Esterházy Collection, 1870

In the nineteenth century most pictures painted with strong effects of light and shade were attributed to Caravaggio, and so was *The Card-Players*, according to the inventory of the Esterházy Collection. Later it was listed as a Bartolomeo Manfredi. The name of Régnier was first suggested in connection with this Budapest picture by Roberto Longhi. According to the German painter-chronicler, Joachim von Sandrart, Régnier was known for his genre paintings in the "Manfrediana method", that is in Manfredi's manner. *The Card-Players* include every characteristic figure of the Roman "Bohemia" of the age: courtesans, thieves, soldiers, the inevitable fortune-teller, and the dissolute young nobleman who is their victim. The painter was rightly regarded by his contemporaries as "naturalistic", for the subject of his pictures was taken from his real surroundings. His style is closely related to that of his two French contemporaries, Valentin and Vouet, even in the choice of types. There is a sense of perfect calm in the composition. The light pouring into the dim room from the left illuminates the sitting figures, forming the shape of a W. Within it the surfaces gleam with the smoothness of porcelain, while the shadows in the folds of the clothes seem to be impressed into the picture. In Régnier's painting this profligate company nonetheless creates a refined and even appealing impression through the curious, sad, meditative expression of the figures. From those of his pictures known to us today it appears that Regnier's mature works, enriched by Bolognese and Venetian influences, never reached the same poetic expression and depth of feeling.

9 NICOLAS RÉGNIER

THE CARD-PLAYERS (detail)

The young man sitting in the foreground—in type related to Vouet's David in Genoa—is one of the main figures in the scene. He looks like the "prodigal son" whom the party is trying to fleece of his money. They can do it all the more easily as the youth is paying no attention to his companions; he not only turns his head away, but in his fine features and his sad, almost tragic expression there seems to be a certain longing. His mind is somewhere else, in a dream-world not known to us, which has taken possession of him and holds him in a kind of trance.

NICOLAS RÉGNIER

THE CARD-PLAYERS (detail)

The model of the provocatively dressed young woman in red is probably identical with that of Saint Irene healing Saint Sebastien in the picture by Régnier in Rouen. She also appears several times in Vouet's pictures, in the *Lovers*, of the Pallavicini Collection in Rome and in *Judith*, in the Kunsthistorisches Museum in Vienna. The sad look in the black eyes, opened wide, in the beautiful face framed by small curls, do not suggest amusement of carefree pleasure, but an immense and all-pervading sadness. The painter seeks out and reveals the depths of the human soul with great power of poetic expression; in this he follows the example of his compatriot, Valentin, but instead of Valentin's dramatic tone his pictures display a tendency towards a certain elegiac tenderness.

11

NICOLAS TOURNIER (?)
1590–after 1657

A Party

Inv. No. 624
Canvas, 125.5 × 170.5 cm
From the Esterházy Collection, 1870

The art of Nicolas Tournier has been hidden by the mists of time to an even greater extent than that of his French contemporaries. Until only a short time ago most of his pictures were still attributed to Valentin and Manfredi. Like Valentin and Régnier, with whose style he has a great deal in common, he too began his career under the influence of Manfredi, and gradually worked his way towards Vouet. Valentin's all-pervading melancholy, however, is absent from his work, which also lacks the tremendous tension to be seen in Vouet's early paintings. The atmosphere is calm and intimate; in this respect, among all the French followers of Caravaggio, he is most closely connected with Georges de La Tour.

In this picture of a company at table Tournier paints the same type, carries on the tradition handed down by Caravaggio and made popular by Bartolommeo Manfredi. The relaxed attitudes of the company blend happily with the sense of intimacy so often found in Tournier's paintings; it frequently verges on a religious emotion, and in this again is akin to the feeling in Georges de La Tour's works.

The picture in Budapest is identical with, but slightly inferior to the version in the City Art Gallery of St. Louis.

MICHEL GOBIN
Active about 1681

Boy Smoking a Pipe

Inv. No. 66.20
Oak panel, 72 × 118 cm
Purchased from a Budapest private collection in 1966

This painting of a youth in Turkish costume, seen in the reddish light of a floating wick, was bought by the Budapest Museum as the work of an unknown master. He was identified by F. G. Pariset as the little-known painter of the second half of the seventeenth century, Michel Gobin. Gobin is believed to have been an artist from Orléans, since three of his pictures have been found there in the last century, all dated 1681. One was a portrait which has since been lost, the other a still-life and the third a composition with figures. His œuvre, as it is known today, consists mainly of still-life subjects which copy or imitate the compositions of the contemporary French painter, Meiffrem Conte. Pariset also discovered foreign inspiration, presumably the influence of Georges de La Tour in his signed picture *The Singing Boy* (Orléans, Museum), inferior in quality to the work in Budapest. Nor are borrowed elements of style lacking in the *Boy Smoking a Pipe;* the fine transitions of light from brown to vermilion are very characteristic of La Tour's scale of colours. On the other hand the elongated form of the composition, the relation between the figure and the interior, and the type of the face indicate the influence of Trophime Bigot, another of Caravaggio's followers. Trophime Bigot, who has only recently been rescued from oblivion, frequently painted turbaned figures, and Gobin follows this practice in both his Budapest and Orléans pictures, even enhancing the exotic character of the costume. In view of the fact that Gobin's still-life paintings appear to be related in style to the work of Meiffrem Conte of Aix-en-Provence, and that the elements in his compositions with figures recall Bigot—who worked in that province—there is every probability that Gobin's work took its roots from southern French, Provençal painting.

NICOLAS POUSSIN (?)
1594–1665

The Rest on the Flight into Egypt

Painted at the end of the 1620s
Inv. No. 57.18
Canvas, 57 × 74 cm
Purchased from a Budapest private collection, 1957
Said to have been in the possession of the Principessa della Cisterna; came up for sale at a Venice auction with the collection of Princess Felicità La Masa (Bevilaqua). Later in the collections of Ferdinando Ongania and Sándor Lederer

This painting, with its frolicking children, radiates a sense of calm and serenity. In a scenery half-screened by hanging drapery, St. Joseph stands absorbed in his book. In the foreground the Madonna tenderly watches the Child on her lap playing with the small Saint John the Baptist. The children on the left of the picture, busy picking fruit and playing at bo-peep, show no signs of the exhaustion evident in the relaxing parents. The style of the picture suggests Poussin's early Roman period. It shows considerable similarity to *The Rest on the Flight into Egypt* in the Karlsruhe Kunsthalle and *Rinaldo and Armida* in Dulwich, although the lighting of the Budapest painting is more restrained and less brilliant. The gentle, poetic tone of the picture is not unknown in Poussin's work, and is found especially in the paintings dating from the first stage of his stay in Rome. It was nevertheless precisely this touch in the style of the picture which raised suspicions over its attribution to Poussin. Those doubts were supported by certain formal shortcomings of the work, above all by the lack of proportion in the drawing of the *putti*, and the exaggerated plumpness of their arms and legs.

The past twenty years have brought many results in a more faithful reconstruction of Poussin's œuvre. Several inferior works, which fail to tally completely with the master's style have been excluded, and at the same time attempts have been made to identify the true authors of the rejected pictures. Doris Wild attributes the Budapest version of *The Rest on the Flight into Egypt* to Charles Mellin, while Anthony Blunt believes it to be the work of another, unknown painter whom he has named "The Master of the Clumsy Children". In fact the picture is related to the style of Poussin's works painted around 1627; its idyllic tranquillity bears witness to the inspiration the young Poussin had found in the harmony of Raphael. Although his paintings have been very richly documented, his work during the period preceding his arrival in Rome is completely unknown, and even his first years in that city are more or less wrapped in obscurity. In any case, the details in the style of the Budapest picture referred to above must caution us in the identification of its authorship.

CLAUDE LORRAIN (CLAUDE GELLÉE)

VILLA IN THE ROMAN CAMPAGNA (detail)

The figures in Claude's landscapes, small as they are in size and proportion, are by no means unimportant. They are not classicistic in drawing, he does not follow any antique models, but in a general way observes the realities of the world, though without elaborating on details. His figures chime perfectly not only with the subject matter and the formal construction of the landscape in which they are to be found, but with its atmosphere as a whole. The light of the setting sun gleams on the figure of the shepherd, and on the cows and goats jogging before him. These simple beings make their way through a noble and unchanging countryside, reminding us of the contrast between the evanescence of man and the enduring stability of nature. The harmony between the figures and forms express one of the fundamental poetic ideas of beauty and peace of a pastoral existence.

GASPARD DUGHET
1615–1675

PASTORAL LANDSCAPE

Painted in the 1650s
Inv. No. 53.490
Canvas, 48.5 × 63.5 cm
Transferred from the Municipal Gallery, 1953; bequeathed by Jenő Zichy; previously in the Viennese collection
of Ödön Zichy

His insistent independence and his passionate love for nature were, according to written
accounts, Dughet's outstanding characteristics. In this painting his favourite view, in the
neighbourhood of Rome, is closed by a group of buildings in the background. The waterfall
dropping from the rocky cleft on the left and the clump of shrubs corner—details reminiscent
of Tivoli—are typical of Dughet in evoking the romantic in nature. "He was not content with
making drawings and studies after nature like so many other landscape painters", wrote
Mariette in the eighteenth century, "but painted most of his pictures directly from nature.
A small donkey, which was his only domestic animal, carried his equipment and a tent, so that
he could paint in a shaded place, sheltered from the wind. He was often to be seen so, spending
whole days in the vicinity of Rome." The Budapest picture is fresh and direct, despite its worn
surface. Marco Chiarini, who puts the picture in the 1650s, mentions a similar painting, dif-
fering only in small details, in an English private collection.

LAURENT DE LA HYRE
1606–1656

THESEUS AND AETHRA

Painted during the late 1630s.
Inv. No. 693
Canvas, 174×135.5 cm
From the Esterházy Collection, 1870

Richelieu, it is well known, commissioned La Hyre to paint three pictures for the Palais Cardinal. The subject of one of them was the same mythological scene as this picture: Theseus, following his mother's instructions, finds the sandals and sword of his father, Aegeus, hidden under a heavy stone. Thuillier's assumption that the picture in Budapest is identical with the one painted for Richelieu is in all likelihood correct, and appears to be also confirmed by the style of the painting.

La Hyre was given the commission towards the end of the 1630s, around the time he painted two pictures, for Notre-Dame, *Peter Healing the Sick* (1635), and *Conversion of Paul* (1637). Numerous peculiarities of style in these works suggest that they are related to the picture in Budapest; among them are the manneristic fine hands, the figures of the women, recalling Blanchard, the softly modelled motifs painted in light, gleaming patches, and last but not least, the extremely fine pale purple colour combinations. (The shape and details of the tree in the background, painted lightly, are repeated in an engraving by La Hyre dated 1640.) The whole character of the picture is one of youthful freshness and spontaneity, of the "Baroque lyricism" of the 1630s which connects the work of La Hyre's early career with Vouet and Blanchard despite the differences of style.

LAURENT DE LA HYRE

Cornelia Rejecting the Crown of the Ptolemies

Painted in 1646
Inv. No. 694
Canvas, 138 × 123 cm
Signed bottom left: HIRE in F. 1646
From the Esterházy Collection, 1870

While Theseus and Aethra represents La Hyre in his most sweeping style, the second picture by this painter in the Budapest Collection—painted at the age of forty—shows the change in his work towards a cooler, more deliberate, and scholarly manner of expression. The carefully researched archaeological details, such as the Gracchus quotation on the tympanum, the sphynx, and the hieroglyphics painted on the flag of the ambassadors, enabled experts to correct the original description of the subject which the Esterházy inventory described as Ninus and Semiramis—the subject of a similar scene. The picture under discussion represents the moment when, according to Roman historians, Cornelia, the daughter of Scipio Africanus, the widow of the Consul Tiberius Gracchus, and the mother of Tiberius and Caius Gracchus, a matron famous for her noble character, rejected the crown and the marriage proposals of Ptolemy, King of Egypt. La Hyre, who was on friendly terms with Abraham Bosse, well-known for his theories on perspective, set his figures, classic in their profile and their posture, in a carefully designed architectural perspective. The figures are clearly and steadily outlined, and this manner of painting, together with the many horizontal and vertical details of the buildings, gives the whole composition a tranquil and dignified effect. Perfection, simplicity and grace, achieved without obvious effort and expressing the ideal in human attitudes and the supremacy of intellect over sentiment, in addition to a strict discipline of form, make the picture a characteristic example of the trend in style which was gaining strength in French painting in the middle of the century. Art historians regard La Hyre's refined painting, with its stress on intellectual and moral qualities as an embodiment of the values implicit in the plays of Corneille and Racine.

NICOLAS LOIR
1624–1679

CLEOBIS AND BITON

Painted around 1649
Inv. No. 698
Canvas, 61 × 74 cm
From the Esterházy Collection, 1870

According to his biographer, Nicolas Loir was a pupil of Sébastien Bourdon, and later completed his training in Italy, from 1647 to 1649. Félibien—who was his friend and travelling companion—mentions him in his *Entretiens sur les vies et les ouvrages des plus excellents peintres...* declaring that he loved Poussin's work but, although he found special pleasure in his paintings he never copied his or any other artist's style. We also know from Félibien that after his return to Paris Loir became very popular among the connoisseurs with his small canvases. *Cleobis and Biton* was among the earliest of these small compositions. He painted it for a friend of his named Lenoir. In addition to the picture in Budapest, another by Loir on the same subject, but larger, is in the Czernin Collection (at present in Salzburg). This story of filial love has been told by several classical authors, among them Herodotos and Plutarch. As the oxen had not returned in time from ploughing, two youths of Argos, Cleobis and Biton themselves pulled their mother's chariot to the temple of Juno for her to make her sacrifice. Loir constructed the picture with its numerous figures with academic care, encompassing the scene in an architectural setting and suggesting perspective by faint, vaporous atmosphere reminiscent of Bourdon. His paintings are full of delicacy, grace and charm, and his slim figures evoke the elegance of the Fontainebleau School.

FRENCH PAINTER OF THE 17TH-CENTURY
(after Raymond Lafage [?])

THE BUILDING OF NOAH'S ARK

2nd half of the 17th century
Inv. No. 9984
Canvas, 158.5 × 109 cm
Transferred from the Budapest Revenue Office, 1950
Counterpart of Plate 31

The composition and spatial arrangement of this picture, painted in clear, cool colours, bears all the marks of the seventeenth-century academic system. In the dramatically vivid figures and their vigorous movements the painter exploits the muscular structure of the human body to the full, stressing the modelling by the use of light and shade. The powerful figures reveal his familiarity with the antique and their animated and straining movements remind one of Michelangelo. This is also an element in the painter's style indicating the attribution of the picture to Lafage, whose affinity with the passionate spirit of Michelangelo has long been recognized; he has often been called "the Michelangelo of Toulouse". The figures in this picture also recall those in Lafage's drawings, above all the short-nosed, broad, bony features of his late self-portrait in the British Museum. The delicate lines of the cypresses and pines in the distant background, just as the freely grouped relics of Roman antiquity in its counterpart, are reminiscent of Italy.

JEAN-BAPTISTE VAN LOO
1684–1745

APOLLO AND DAPHNE

From the Paris years of the artist (1720–1737)
Inv. No. 3833
Canvas, 157 × 127.5 cm
Purchased from Goudstikker, art dealer in Amsterdam 1908; previously in the Prague collection of G. Hoschek von Mühlheim

Jean-Baptiste van Loo was a member of a large family of artists. His younger brother, Carl van Loo, was one of the most popular decorative painters of the age; the development of his elegant and easy style was partly due to the influence of Jean-Baptiste, who began to study painting in his father's studio in Aix-en-Provence, and later went to Italy, where he worked in Rome, Genoa and Turin. He settled in Paris in 1720, became in 1731 a member and later a professor of the Academy there. Like many of his contemporaries he worked a long time abroad, spending his last years in England, and consequently helped to spread the eighteenth-century French style of painting in Europe. He became the favourite portrait painter of the French court, and he also produced paintings on mythological subjects. This picture is one of a series of twelve painted for the Duke of Perpignan. Apollo's tragic love for Daphne and her persecution by the god, seen in the act of turning her into a tree, is painted by the artist in a limpid, easy-flowing manner. The variegated and decorative background setting of the graceful rhythm of the figures, and the gentle gradations of light and shade are typical of the pleasant, somewhat facile style which earned Jean-Baptiste van Loo his popularity.

JEAN-BAPTISTE SIMÉON CHARDIN
1699–1779

STILL-LIFE WITH TURKEY

A late work of the painter
Inv. No. 8898
Canvas, 96 × 113 cm
Signed at bottom left: Chardin
Acquired in 1948; previously in the collections of Lipót Herzog and Marcell Nemes

When Chardin showed his still-life canvases at the Academy, Largillière believed them to be Flemish, and was greatly surprised to learn that they were the works of a young Frenchman. His contemporaries and predecessors had only used still-life objects as decorative elements, and Chardin's simple and familiar treatment of "dead things" created an unusual impression. The effect produced by these common objects of everyday life, in the gentle light that pervades his pictures is not, either exclusively or primarily, due to their outward appearance, but rather to their inner essence, the suggestion of their relationship with humanity, creating an intimate and poetic world only perhaps comparable to that of the Le Nain Brothers. Throughout his long career the objects he painted remained much the same, copper pans scattered on the kitchen table, a glass, baskets of fruit, and game represented his whole artistic universe. The means he employed changed little and slowly, in the course of his career, mostly in the direction of greater simplification. Light played a major role among them. The use of light is his most important method of construction; through the reflection of light the objects are firmly placed and given their spatial meaning. With the progress of time his brush-work became rougher: in the manner of applying colours he obtained an almost Pointillist effect. His *Still-life with Turkey* is painted with a subtle palette running from white through shades of red to deep brown. The silver of the turkey melts into its surrounding in a series of soft gradations of colour, nothing is strongly accentuated; peaceful quiet of familiar life reigns in a world in which the inanimate objects are deeply imbued with a sense of the world surrounding them.

PIERRE BERNARD

PORTRAIT OF A YOUNG WOMAN

Painted in 1763
Inv. No. 63.18
Pastel on paper, 50×40 cm
Signed at bottom left: Bernard pinx.
Bought from a private collection in Budapest, 1963; previously in the Forgács (Lipthay) Castle at Szécsény (Hungary)
Counterpart of Plate 39

Pierre Bernard made a name for himself in the same period that saw the activities of the greatest master of pastel portraits, Maurice Quentin de La Tour. Compared to De La Tour, his technique is less polished, but the roughness of his surfaces, his more "painterly" application of the pastel stick, only enhance his originality. Compared to his other well-known works, especially to the portraits of the Imperial family dating from the same year, the Budapest pictures are simple and unaffected. There is no deep psychological insight in his work, nor any expression of patrician hauteur. He devotes immense care and skill to the decorative painting of fine materials, furs, velvets and lace, as can be seen in his *Portrait of a Young Woman*.

JEAN-FRANÇOIS-PIERRE PEYRON
1744–1814

KING PERSEUS BEFORE AEMILIUS PAULUS

Painted in 1802
Inv. No. 662
Walnut panel, 32 × 46 cm
Signed at bottom right on step of the throne:
P. Peyron inv. et f. 1802
From the Esterházy Collection, 1870

Peyron chose an episode from ancient history as the subject of his picture, but he was more interested in its moral significance than in the historical event itself.

Ignobly fearing for his life, wrote Plutarch, Perseus, the defeated King, prostrated himself before the victorious Aemilius Paulus begging for mercy, but his self-abasement only provoked words of disdain and scorn from the military leader. "In the eyes of the Romans valour wins esteem for the enemy," he said, "even if they meet with misfortune, but cowardice only provokes our contempt, even if it brings luck to the coward."

This composition painted almost as if in relief, his figures shaped with sculptural plasticity, form a link between the works of Poussin and David. Like David, Peyron studied under Joseph Marie Vien, whose graceful style was transformed by his pupils into a stricter formal idiom. The heroic attitude implicit in Peyron's picture and its deep, dark colours are comparable to David's; to match his crystal clear style all Peyron needed was the final coherence of genius.

42

GABRIEL-FRANÇOIS DOYEN
1726–1806

Juno and Aeolus (The Allegory of Air; detail)

Painted in 1753
Inv. No. 60.8
Canvas, 355 × 217 cm
Signed at bottom right: GF Doyen 1753
Purchased in 1960; previously in the Esterházy Collection

Paul Anton Esterházy was Ambassador in Naples from 1750 to 1752 and there his wife commissioned art students of the French Academy of Rome to paint allegorical pictures of the four elements, Water, Fire, Earth and Air. The painters entrusted with the work were respectively Charles-François de La Traverse, Pierre-Charles Mettay, Jean Barbault, and Doyen. Only one of the pictures, Doyen's *Air*, published by Klára Garas, is known at present, the other three have either perished or their whereabouts are unknown.

As a student of the French Academy in Rome, Doyen had given long study to the Italian masters, and the picture in Budapest, a large work from his early period, shows the elemental effect the formal language of Italian Baroque exercised on his style. His treatment of the subject shows no trace of the superficial facility that had become so fashionable in French decorative painting. His massive figures and the great crowds counterposed against vivid juxtapositions of light and shade, painted with all the vigour of a Rubens give the mythological subject a rhetorical dignity that recalled to his contemporaries the *grand goût* (taste for grandeur) of earlier times. Diderot, who was never slow to attack the "frivolity" of contemporary painting, was enthusiastic, and spoke in terms of high praise of the gravity and convincing power of Doyen's style, extolling him as the man who had restored the painterly qualities proper to French art before the "decline". Doyen, with his powerful and dynamic manner of painting was the precursor of Géricault, the great romantic of the nineteenth century, a clear demonstration of the faculty of French painting to span stylistic periods and renew itself. Doyen's picture is painted on a very large canvas, and we are only able to reproduce a detail showing Aeolus as he frees the Winds by Juno's command.

JEAN-BAPTISTE GREUZE

Portrait of a Young Girl

Painted between 1650 and 1700
Inv. No. 53.390
Canvas, 50×38 cm
Signed right centre: J. B. Greuze
Transferred from the Municipal Gallery, 1953; bequeathed by Jenő Zichy; previously in the Viennese collection of Ödön Zichy

The pale face of the young girl, shaped somewhat like a mask, with its half open lips, stands out against the deep shades of the background glancing back enigmatically over her shoulder. It is a typical portrait of Greuze. By slightly exaggerating the sentimental and theatrical elements, he approaches genre painting.

45

LOUIS-LÉOPOLD BOILLY
1761–1845

VISITING GRANDFATHER

Painted in the 2nd half of the 18th century
Inv. No. 687
Walnut panel, 24.7 × 32.5 cm
From the Esterházy Collection. Purchased in 1816

The Netherlands did not only leave their impress on French painting through Rubens and Rembrandt: the influence of the "lesser masters" was also continuous from the seventeenth to the end of the eighteenth and even into the nineteenth century. The carefully elaborated style affected by Boilly, his porcelain-smooth surfaces and meticulous technique, removing every trace of the brush-stroke, recall the overstudied, polished Dutch style of painting, the *Feinmalerei*, of the end of the seventeenth century. There is a certain sentimentality, inspired by Greuze, in his glibly painted narrative scenes and conversation pieces.

46

ADRIEN MANGLARD
(1695—1760)

ESTUARY WITH HARBOUR

In the first half of the 17th century
Inv. No. 680
Canvas, 55 × 98 cm
Signed bottom right: Manglard
From the Esterházy Collection, 1870

The seascape came into fashion in Rome at the beginning of the seventeenth century, and was first introduced there by Dutch painters living in Italy. Claude Lorrain and Salvator Rosa, the two greatest landscape painters in Italy at the time, took over this peculiarly Netherlandish form of art, and were followed by others, who continued to paint seascapes well into the eighteenth century. Adrien Manglard, who came to Italy as a young man, was one of them. Although he remained in contact with the artistic life of Paris, he never returned to France. He specialized in seascapes, became a professor at the Accademia di San Luca in Rome, and also produced a large number of paintings and drawings devoted to this subject. His scenes, adorned with a wealth of genre detail, were greatly appreciated by Goethe.

He was interested above all in the sunrise and sunset effects of light seen through sea mists, the basic problem interesting Claude Lorrain as well. But in Manglard's seascapes it is not the majestic calm of the scene which dominates, but the busting activities of everyday life suggested by his gesturing figures and hinting at the influence of Salvator Rosa.

In this picture the sunlight is broken and almost absorbed by the mist enveloping the busy harbour. In the careful construction of space and perspective the painter has attached more importance to the comparative sizes of the figures placed along different planes than to the gradations of the aerial perspective.

47

JOSEPH VERNET
(1714—1789)

VIEW WITH CASTLE RUINS

Painted before 1756
Inv. No. 674
Canvas, 48×64 cm
From the Esterházy Collection, 1870

Among the French painters of the eighteenth century the artist most influenced by Claude Lorrain was the landscape painter Joseph Vernet. After a successful beginning as a painter in Avignon he continued his career in Italy, only returning to France some twenty years later. Diderot praised the pictures he exhibited at the *Salon*s. His enthusiastic description of Vernet's work, although his views may not always tally with ours, is extremely characteristic of the age and the change in taste that had taken place: "...(Vernet) ...is Claude's equal... and even surpasses him in the execution and variety of his scenes and figures. Claude is simply a great landscape painter but, to my mind, Vernet is a 'history-painter'." This was the greatest praise a French painter could be given, since according to the scale of values set up by the Academy, the "historical painter" had for a century been placed in the highest category. The variety in his scenes so enthusiastically praised by Diderot in his review of the 1765 *Salon* referred to the descriptive character and "literary" inspiration of Vernet's landscapes and other types of paintings. In this picture a huge cave framing the view opens on a moonlit scene emerging in vague and mysterious silhouette against the moonlit sky, the whole painted in various tones of brown.

48

HUBERT ROBERT
(1733—1808)

RUINS WITH FIGURES

From the artist's Italian period (1754—1765)
Inv. No. 655
Paper, 32,8 × 24,8 cm
Signed on the base of the obelisk: H. Robert
From the Esterházy Collection, 1870; purchased from the bequest of J. Fischer, Director of the Gallery

Hubert Robert spent eleven years in Italy. The inexhaustible variety of the Italian landscape with its ruins and relics of antiquity exercised a greater influence on him than on any of the Italian painters. His landscapes—the form of art to which his whole life was dedicated— are filled with monuments and ancient buildings conveying the grandeur of the past. The details are fresh and direct, rather than archaeologically accurate. The subject of the small masterpiece in Budapest is quite unassuming: an ox-cart passing under some great arch of antiquity, overgrown with ivy, and on the right of the canvas weary wayfarers resting beside a broken obelisk. The picture is painted in strong contrasts of light and shade with fast strokes of the brush, producing surface recalling Fragonard, his travelling companion in Italy. "Why is it that a beautiful sketch pleases us more than a beautiful picture?" asks Diderot. And replies: "Because there is more life and less form in it. The sketch is the work of the genius." In this painting of Robert's the vibrant brush-strokes seem to sway with the wind-driven clouds in the sky, yet despite the movement of the brush a sense of contemplative poetry and peace floats over the whole painting.